CRIMPiT

100+ CRIMPiT Wrap Recipe Ideas

First published September 2023
Published by Independent Publishing Network

CRIMPiT Group LTD

45 Fitzroy Street, 4th Floor,
Silverstream House,
London, England,
W1T 6EB

crimpit.com

Please direct all enquiries to the author -
support@crimpit.com

ISBN 978-1-7395618-0-2

Printed in United Kingdom

100+ CRIMPiT Wrap Recipe Ideas

Facebook thecrimpit

Instagram the_crimpit

TikTok the_crimpit

CRIMPiT

CONTENTS

Intro	6 - 7
How to use your CRIMPiT Wrap	8 - 9
Heating your CRIMPiT Wrap	10 - 11
Meat	12 - 59
Fish	60 - 73
Vegetarian	74 - 101
Vegan	102 - 111
Sweet	112 - 122

CRIMPiT

Congratulations on buying your CRIMPiT Wrap. You are now only a few steps away from creating delicious snacks. The CRIMPiT Wrap is extremely versatile and is only limited by your imagination.

You can literally put any ingredients in that you like. You can use wraps or pastry it's up to you! Just make sure you cook any raw ingredients before adding. Then you can warm your snack in an air fryer, oven, grill or pan.

Now you have a whole new way to enjoy wraps like you've never seen them before. Happy Crimping!

HOW TO USE YOUR CRIMPiT

How To Create The Perfect Crimpit Wrap

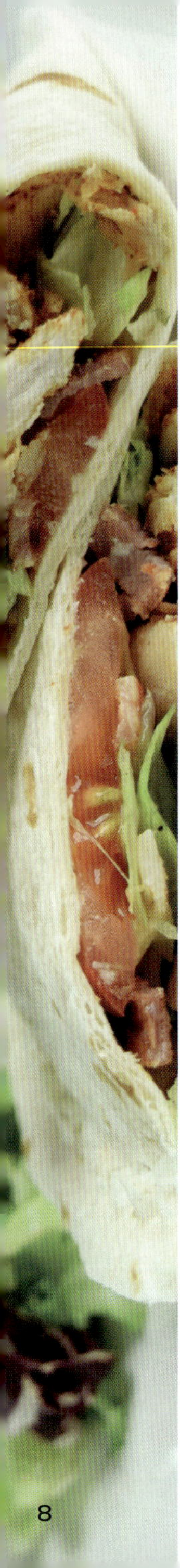

- Buy your favourite Wraps. Available at all major supermarkets.

- Place your Wrap over the CRIMPiT, then add your favourite fillings. Leave a little space around the edge of the Wrap.

- Place the CRIMPiT into the microwave for 20 seconds to soften the Wrap ready for crimping.

- If you don't have a microwave, you can wet a finger and run it around the edge, the water acts as a glue in helping the wrap stick together.
- Remove from the microwave, fold over your Wrap then close the CRIMPiT lid and squeeze together.
- Open the CRIMPiT and take out the sealed CRIMPiT parcel. You can now heat the crimped parcel however you like! Air fryer, grill, oven, dry fry in a pan or enjoy it cold.

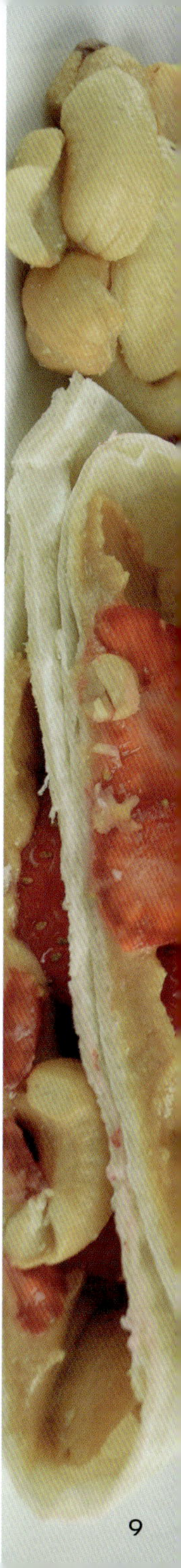

NINJA
TEMP
TIME
AIR FRY
ROAST
REHEAT
DEHYDRATE
START/STOP

HEATING YOUR CRIMPiT

All cooking appliances vary therefore, these are only provisional guidelines.

In the Pan	6 Minutes
In the air fryer	200°C on air fry for 4 minutes
In the oven	200°C / gas 7 for 6 minutes

Please ensure you do not heat the plastic device. All food should be removed before heating.

HEATING YOUR PASTRY CRIMPiT

Cook pastry as per packet instructions using your air fryer or oven. Make sure pastry is cooked before eating.

MEAT

LOADED BREAKFAST WRAP

Ingredients

700-800 KCAL

50g Cooked sausage

30g Cooked bacon

2 Scrambled eggs

30g Baked beans

20g Cooked mushrooms

30g Tomato sauce

Chef's Tip

Use streaky smoked bacon and chipolata sausages to give you the perfect start to the morning. If you want an extra bit of zing, add a few drops of tabasco.

SCRAMBLED EGG & BACON

Ingredients

KCAL 850-900

3 Scrambled eggs

50g Cooked bacon

35g Tomato

30g Tomato sauce

Chef's Tip

Sprinkle grated cheese on top of the crimped wrap before cooking for extra flavour.

BLT

Ingredients

KCAL
450-500

60g Cooked bacon

40g Shredded lettuce

50g Sliced tomato

40g Mayonnaise

5g Parsley

Chef's Tip

Add caesar dressing instead of mayo for an enhanced flavour. Enjoy cold for packed lunches and picnics.

SAUSAGE, BEAN & CHEESE

Ingredients

KCAL 510-560

70g Cooked sausage

50g Baked beans

40g Grated cheese

30g Brown sauce

Chef's Tip

Try experimenting with different sausages. Pork and apple, lamb and mint or spicy beef.

SERRANO HAM, BLUE CHEESE & PEAR

Ingredients

KCAL 350-400

55g Jamon serrano

40g Sliced pear

40g Blue cheese

20g Rocket

20g Cream cheese

Chef's Tip

You can replace jamon serrano with your preferred cured meat and enjoy hot or cold.

CALZONE

Ingredients

KCAL
650-700

60g Sliced salami

50g Shredded mozzarella

50g Pizza sauce

5g Fresh basil

100g Pizza dough

Chef's Tip

You can use store bought dough or make your own. Replace any ingredients with your own to create the perfect calzone.

BACON, CHEESE, ONION & PICKLES

Ingredients

KCAL 350-400

50g Cooked bacon

50g Sliced cheddar

40g Red onion

40g Pickles

Chef's Tip

Try a different type of pickle, such as, pickled onions, gherkins, and piccalilli to mix up your CRIMPiT.

CLASSIC ROAST BEEF

Ingredients

KCAL 150-200

60g Sliced roast beef

30g Horseradish sauce

15g Watercress

60g Leftover roast vegetables

Chef's Tip

Use up your leftover roast dinner to create this perfect CRIMPiT. Enjoy hot or cold.

MINTED ROAST LAMB

Ingredients

KCAL
350-400

70g Flaked roast lamb

30g Tender stem broccoli

30g Yoghurt

15g Mint sauce

20g Rocket

Chef's Tip

Add spices and pomegranate seeds to give this a Moroccan feel.

PORK AND APPLE

Ingredients

KCAL 230-270

80g Roast pork

30g Apple sauce

25g Pickled red cabbage

25g Tender stem broccoli

10g Sliced apple

7g Dijon mustard

Chef's Tip

Ingredients can also be replaced with those from a leftover pork meal. Mix the vegetables with the apple sauce for maximum flavour.

CHICKEN CAESAR

Ingredients

KCAL
350-400

60g Cooked chicken

10g Chopped cooked bacon

30g Cucumber

15g Sun dried tomato

15g Cream cheese

15g Baby gem lettuce

20g Caesar dressing

Chef's Tip

Replace bacon with salted peanuts to keep the salty crunch and save time cooking bacon.

CHEESE BURGER

Ingredients

KCAL
400-500

80g Cooked beef mince or burger

40g Grated cheese

25g Sliced pickles

30g Burger sauce

10g Red onion

Chef's Tip

Add any additional favourite burger toppings to the recipe to create your ultimate crimped burger!

CHICKEN CURRY

Ingredients

300-350 KCAL

55g Cooked chicken thigh

30g Coconut yoghurt

5g Curry powder

30g Mango chutney

15g Sliced onion

30g Cooked rice

5g Fresh coriander

Chef's Tip

To add a bit of spice, add crushed red chillies and curry leaves.

ITALIAN SALAD

Ingredients

KCAL
300-350

60g Prosciutto

40g Sun dried tomato

40g Sliced Italian cheese

20g Black Olives

15g Shredded lettuce

Chef's Tip

Fresh basil and balsamic glaze will add an extra level of flavour to this recipe.

CORONATION CHICKEN

Ingredients

KCAL 300-350

60g Cooked chicken

25g Cheddar

25g Mayonnaise

10g Raisins

5g Pine nuts

15g Rocket

1 tbs Curry powder

Chef's Tip

Try adding cucumber for an added crunch.

CHICKEN & AVOCADO

Ingredients

KCAL
350-400

80g Grilled chicken breast

45g Avocado

25g Mayonnaise

30g Sun dried tomato

Chef's Tip

Add red onions and asparagus for an extra crunch. Try some chilli flakes for added spice.

BUFFALO CHICKEN

Ingredients

KCAL 250-300

65g Grilled chicken breast

5g Buffalo seasoning

30g Ranch dressing

20g Crispy bacon

20g Chopped tomatoes

20g Lettuce

Chef's Tip

Not a fan of ranch dressing? Try blue cheese instead.

SATAY CHICKEN

Ingredients

KCAL 150-200

70g Cooked satay chicken

30g Grated carrot

35g Cucumber

20g Lettuce

5g Coriander

Chef's Tip

Satay sauce can be bought or made. Add extra peanuts for a bigger crunch.

STEAK AND CHEESE

Ingredients

KCAL
320-370

75g Cooked steak

30g Caramelised onion

35g Cheddar

25g Cooked mushrooms

20g Cream cheese

Chef's Tip

Cook the onion and steak together for maximum flavour. If you're rushed for time, use jarred onion.

TEX MEX CHICKEN

Ingredients

65g Cooked chicken

25g Chipotle sauce

40g Crushed black beans

40g Cooked peppers

20g Red onion

5g Coriander

KCAL

280-330

Chef's Tip

Add grated cheddar and jalapeños to enhance the Mexican flavour.

CHORIZO, TOMATO, OLIVE & MOZZARELLA

Ingredients

KCAL 350-400

55g Chorizo

30g Tomato

15g Olives

30g Mozzarella

30g Hummus

Chef's Tip

If you don't like spice, replace chorizo with your favourite cured meat such as salami.

CHILLI CON CARNE & SOUR CREAM

Ingredients

80g Beef chilli

10g Spinach

20g Sour cream

25g Cheddar

5g Paprika

25g Jalapeños

KCAL 250-300

Chef's Tip

If you're not a fan of sour cream, try adding some plain yoghurt.

HAWAIIAN HAM

Ingredients

KCAL
200-250

60g Sliced Ham

35g Grated mozzarella

35g Pineapple chunks

20g Cream cheese

Chef's Tip

Try with pizza dough to create the perfect crimped Hawaiian pizza.

CRUNCHY CON CARNE

Ingredients

KCAL 400-500

85g Beef chilli

25g Crushed nachos

40g Cream cheese

5g Coriander

10g Jalapeños

Chef's Tip

Add your favourite grated cheese on top and melt under the grill for a deliciously cheesy glazed wrap.

SHEPHERD'S PIE

Ingredients

KCAL 300-400

85g Cooked minced lamb
(or leftover shepherd's pie)
25g Grated courgette
10g Spinach
15g Mint sauce
25g Yoghurt

Chef's Tip

You can use cooked lamb instead of mince, but why not make extra shepherd's pie and crimp it the next day!

PULLED PORK

Ingredients

65g Pulled pork

40g Spiced mayonnaise

40g Cooked peppers

30g Cucumber

20g Baby gem lettuce

KCAL
550-600

Chef's Tip

If you like an extra kick, try adding dried chilli powder or your favourite hot sauce.

PULLED BEEF & PICKLES

Ingredients

300-400 KCAL

80g Braised/pulled beef

40g Grated cheddar

30g Sliced pickled gherkins

40g Sauerkraut

Chef's Tip

Sauerkraut can be found in most supermarkets and adds a different pickled flavour. Pulled beef can be replaced with cured beef such as bresaola.

PHILLY CHEESESTEAK

Ingredients

KCAL
260-310

65g Pastrami

40g Sliced gherkins

30g Cheddar cheese

20g Dijon mustard

30g White sauce

Chef's Tip

If you don't have a white sauce, use cream cheese instead.

SMOKED TURKEY & COLESLAW

Ingredients

KCAL
150-200

75g Smoked turkey/turkey ham

45g Coleslaw

20g English mustard

20g Salad leaves

Chef's Tip

Try adding apple for an extra crunch.

SAUSAGE PARTY

Ingredients

KCAL
450-500

40g Pepperoni

40g Cooked sausage

30g Peppers

15g Black olives

15g Red onion

20g Cooked mushrooms

30g Pizza sauce

Chef's Tip

Use pizza dough as a great alternative to a wrap.

ASIAN PORK

Ingredients

KCAL 250-300

70g Cooked pork mince

5g Ginger

5g Garlic

15g Grated carrot

10g Spring onions

15g Baby gem lettuce

10g Soy sauce

25g Sweet chilli sauce

Chef's Tip

Try alternative veggies such as zucchini & white onion to give the wrap tons of flavour and an extra crunch.

MEATBALLS

Ingredients

80g Cooked Meatballs

40g Cooked pasta

40g Cheese sauce

20g Tomato pasta sauce

KCAL

400-500

Chef's Tip

If you don't have meatballs you can use sausages cut into thick slices.

CHICKEN, BACON & BRIE

Ingredients

KCAL
450-550

75g Cooked chicken

30g Cooked bacon

40g Brie

30g Sweet chilli sauce

Chef's Tip

If you don't like spice, swap out sweet chilli for cranberry sauce. Brie can be replaced with your favourite cheese.

BBQ PORK

Ingredients

70g Braised pork

30g Bbq sauce

20g Sweetcorn

50g Cooked sweet potato

KCAL
300-350

Chef's Tip

You can use any cooked pork to create this recipe. Try adding rice for a more filling meal.

CHICKEN & MUSHROOM PIE

Ingredients

450-550 KCAL

60g Cooked chicken

20g Cooked mushrooms

20g Sweetcorn

50g White sauce

5g Chopped parsley

Puff/Shortcrust pastry

Chef's Tip

Add smoked streaky bacon for added flavour and glaze with egg wash for the perfect golden finish.

CHICKEN AND STUFFING

Ingredients

300-350 KCAL

60g Cooked chicken

40g Cooked stuffing

40g Roast vegetables

25g Cranberry sauce

Chef's Tip

Swap out the vegetables for red onion and tomatoes for a lighter meal.

STEAK AND STILTON

Ingredients

300-350 KCAL

80g Sliced steak

35g Crumbled stilton

25g Tomato

15g Lettuce

1 Tsp Dijon mustard

Chef's Tip

Replace stilton and mustard with your preferred cheese and sauce for your ultimate steak and cheese CRIMPiT.

CHICKEN FAJITA

Ingredients

300-350 KCAL

65g Cooked chicken

5g Fajita seasoning

25g Tomato salsa

25g Guacamole

20g Cooked peppers

30g Grated cheddar

Chef's Tip

You can use fresh tomatoes and diced avocado instead of salsa and guacamole.

CUMIN LAMB, CRUNCHY SLAW & SPICED MAYO

Ingredients

KCAL
350-450

65g Cooked lamb

5g Cumin

30g Chopped cabbage

30g Grated carrot

5g Parsley

30g Mayo

Tabasco to taste

Chef's Tip

Add peppers and spring onions for a loaded meal with an extra crunch.

SALAMI, BAKED BEAN & MOZZARELLA

Ingredients

KCAL
350-450

40g Salami

100g Baked beans

50g Grated mozzarella

30g Tomato

10g Rocket

15g Cream cheese

Chef's Tip

Try swapping the cream cheese for chilli sauce and mustard.

POSH PATE

Ingredients

250-300 KCAL

60g Duck and orange pate

30g Cucumber

30g Carrot

15g Orange

15g Rocket

20g Avocado

10g Pine nuts

Chef's Tip

Serve with baked sweet potatoes or a light salad.

APPLE CHEDDAR & TURKEY

Ingredients

KCAL 300-400

70g Smoked turkey/turkey ham

45g Smoked applewood cheddar

40g Sliced apple

30g Piccalilli

Chef's Tip

Try changing apples with onions for a more savoury taste. Cheddar can be replaced with any of your favourite cheese.

MEXICAN PORK & BLACK BEANS

Ingredients

350-450 KCAL

65g Sliced pork

45g Black bean puree

30g Cooked peppers

20g Red onion

25g Sour cream

30g Mozzarella

5g Coriander

Chef's Tip

Black beans can be purchased, cooked and then crushed or blended to make a puree.

CHICKEN GOUJON

Ingredients

450-500 KCAL

80g Chicken goujons

50g French fries

25g Tomato sauce

30g Spiced mayonnaise

Chef's Tip

Try fish goujons and a squeeze of lemon as different option.

STEAK AND CHIPS

Ingredients

KCAL 450-550

80g Sliced cooked steak

50g French fries

30g Burger sauce

30g Grated cheddar

10g Rocket

Chef's Tip

Swap out fries for sliced onion, mushrooms and tomato for a healthier meal.

PORK & SWISS CHEESE

Ingredients

KCAL
250-350

60g Roast pork

40g Sliced Ham

35g Swiss cheese

20g English mustard

25g Sliced pickles

Chef's Tip

Not a fan of swiss cheese? Try blue cheese, mozzarella or cheddar cheese.

CHORIZO & FRIED EGG

Ingredients

KCAL
600-650

65g Chorizo

2 Fried eggs

30g Cream cheese

15g Spinach

30g Tomato

Chef's Tip

Adding cooked egg is the best way to crimp. They can be fried or scrambled.

FISH

SMOKED SALMON & CREAM CHEESE

Ingredients

KCAL 200-250

65g Smoked salmon

20g Spinach

30g Cucumber

30g Cream cheese

Squeeze of lemon

5g Chopped herbs

Chef's Tip

Try this recipe with tinned tuna if you're looking for a quick meal.

SMOKED SALMON & AVOCADO

Ingredients

300-350 KCAL

70g Smoked salmon

35g Crème fraiche

40g Avocado

30g Tomato

15g Rocket

Chef's Tip

Cream cheese and any lettuce can be used if you do not have crème fraiche or rocket.

SCRAMBLED EGG & SMOKED SALMON

Ingredients

KCAL 250-300

2 Scrambled eggs

60g Smoked salmon

30g Grated Cheddar

15g Spinach

20g Cooked mushrooms

Chef's Tip

Add a splash of lemon juice for an enhanced flavour.

PRAWN MAYO

Ingredients

KCAL
400-450

65g Cooked prawns

40g Avocado

2g Chilli

20g Baby gem lettuce

25g Tomato

25g Lemon mayonnaise

Chef's Tip

Not a big fan of spice? Try using paprika instead of chilli for a less spicy meal.

TUNA MELT

Ingredients

KCAL 250-300

80g Tinned Tuna

20g Mayonnaise

30g Grated mozzarella

20g Red onion

20g Tomato

Chef's Tip

Replace mayo with cream cheese and spicy sauce for a creamy spicy mix.

LIME SHRIMP

Ingredients

KCAL
250-300

70g Cooked prawns

35g Cream cheese

20g Lettuce

½ Lime

20g Tomato

5g Cumin

5g Garlic paste

Chef's Tip

Use any salad ingredients you have to mix with the prawns, lime and cream cheese to build the ultimate prawn wrap.

FISH FINGER WRAP

Ingredients

250-300 KCAL

90g Cooked Fish fingers (3)

35g Tartar sauce

50g Mushy peas

Chef's Tip

Tartar sauce can be made with mayonnaise, lemon, chopped gerkins, shallots, parsley and/or capers.

SMOKED TROUT & BEETROOT

Ingredients

KCAL
150-200

65g Smoked trout

50g Cooked beetroot

30g Tomato

15g Watercress

20g Horseradish

Chef's Tip

Any smoked or cured fish can be used instead of smoked trout to create this tasty treat.

PRAWN FAJITA

Ingredients

KCAL
350-450

65g Cooked prawns

5g Fajita seasoning

35g Avocado

25g Red onion

40g Cooked peppers

25g Cream cheese

Chef's Tip

Try soured cream instead of cream cheese.
Add some chilli if you like extra spice.

TUNA MAYO

Ingredients

80g Tinned tuna
35g Mayonnaise
30g Tomato
30g Avocado
20g Pesto
25g Sliced pickles

KCAL
400-500

Chef's Tip

If you want to enhance the flavours in this recipe, add fresh herbs such as parsley, coriander, or basil.

TERIYAKI SALMON

Ingredients

KCAL 200-250

65g Hot smoked salmon

20g Teriyaki sauce

20g Mange tout

10g Spring onion

25g Edamame

30g Coconut yoghurt

20g Red onion

Squeeze of lemon

Chef's Tip

You can use any yoghurt although coconut adds a different flavour to this recipe.

FISH AND CHIPS

Ingredients

KCAL
450-550

70g Cooked Fish goujons

50g French fries

30g Pesto

30g Edamame beans

20g Lemon mayo

5g Pea shoots

Chef's Tip

Try fish goujons with cucumber and mixed vegetables for a lighter meal. Serve with wedges or mushy peas.

FLAKED HOT SMOKED SALMON & EGG

Ingredients

KCAL
300-350

60g Hot smoked salmon

2 Hard boiled eggs (crushed)

15g Whole grain mustard

20g Mayonnaise

15g Watercress

Chef's Tip

Swap out watercress for cherry tomatoes, cucumber, avocado and spring onions for a loaded wrap.

VEGETARIAN

COURGETTE MARGARITA

Ingredients

KCAL
150-250

30g Pizza sauce

40g Grated courgette

15g Sliced tomato

35g Grated mozzarella

5g Fresh basil

Chef's Tip

Use pizza dough instead of a wrap to make a tasty vegetarian calzone.

ROAST VEGETABLES & GOATS CHEESE

Ingredients

KCAL
150-250

75g Grilled or roast vegetables

30g Goats cheese

10g Rocket

5g Balsamic vinegar

20g Sliced red onion

Chef's Tip

Grilled vegetables work best. If you like pesto, add it to this recipe to enhance all the flavours.

THREE CHEESE & SPINACH

Ingredients

KCAL 300-350

50g 2 of your favourite cheeses

50g Ricotta

30g Shredded spinach

Chef's Tip

Use one soft and one hard cheese for different textures and add fresh herbs to add to the flavour.

CAULIFLOWER CHEESE

Ingredients

KCAL
250-300

65g Cooked cauliflower

40g Cheese sauce

40g Grated mozzarella

30g Grated carrot

15g Spinach

Chef's Tip

Add almonds and breadcrumbs with some extra cheese on top for an added crunch.

MACARONI CHEESE

Ingredients

KCAL
450-550

75g Cooked macaroni

45g Cheese sauce

20g Bread crumbs

30g Sun dried tomato

30g Feta

Chef's Tip

For a more simple recipe, use leftover pasta with plenty of grated cheese, adding any other additional ingredients you like, such as olives, chorizo or tuna.

SPICED POTATO

Ingredients

KCAL
200-250

70g Cooked diced potato

10g Curry spice

10g Garlic and ginger paste

30g Diced peppers

10g Spring onion

15g Lime pickle

25g Cream cheese

Chef's Tip

Use leftover curry from the night before to make this recipe in a few minutes.

ARTICHOKE & BUTTERNUT

Ingredients

KCAL
200-250

60g Artichoke hearts

60g Roast butternut or pumpkin

30g Parmesan

5g Garlic

25g Grated mozzarella

10g Spinach

Chef's Tip

Add a sprinkle of dried chilli to spice things up!

REFRIED BEANS

Ingredients

65g Refried beans

35g Tomato Salsa

20g Sliced red onion

25g Crushed nachos

10g Spring onion

15g Cos lettuce

25g Grated cheddar cheese

30g Chilli mayonnaise

KCAL
280-330

Chef's Tip

Serve with rice and spicy coleslaw for a Mexican style feast.

CORN SALAD

Ingredients

KCAL
200-250

60g Sweetcorn

35g Jalapeños

30g Cooked mushrooms

30g Diced courgette

30g Grated carrot

35g Cheese sauce

20g Tomato salsa

Chef's Tip

Add bbq sauce instead of salsa for a more smokey intense flavour.

AVOCADO SALAD

Ingredients

KCAL 300-350

70g Avocado

20g Lettuce

20g Onion

20g Tomato

20g Cucumber

5g Basil

35g Cream cheese

5g Sliced chilli

Chef's Tip

Add lemon or lime juice to enhance the flavours in this recipe.

FETA AND HUMMUS

Ingredients

350-400 KCAL

50g Feta

40g Sun dried tomato

25g Olives

25g Artichoke

30g Hummus

15g Rocket

5g Paprika

Chef's Tip

Artichoke can be replaced with any vegetable you like, as long as its cooked and ready to eat.

CRUSHED CHICKPEAS

Ingredients

150-200

70g Crushed Chickpeas

5g Fresh mint

25g Yoghurt

35g Cooked red pepper

15g Spinach

Chef's Tip

You can replace the chickpeas with any bean, pea or pulse to suit your taste.

VEGGIE DELIGHT

Ingredients

KCAL
200-250

30g Pickled cabbage

45g Hummus

30g Grated courgette

30g Grated carrot

30g Cooked peppers

20g Mixed salad leaves

Chef's Tip

Swap the vegetables out for your favourites. Balsamic vinegar will add the pickled flavour if you don't have pickled cabbage.

SPICED SWEET POTATO & SPINACH

Ingredients

KCAL 200-250

90g Cooked sweet potato

30g Coconut milk

3g Sesame seeds

5g Curry spice

30g Spinach

20g Onion

Chef's Tip

Add cashew nuts for added protein and an extra crunch.

HALLOUMI & MAPLE

Ingredients

KCAL
480-530

70g Halloumi

30g Maple syrup

30g Aioli

30g Spiced mango ketchup

30g Sliced tomato

40g Baby gem lettuce

Chef's Tip

Fry the haloumi before adding it for extra flavour and texture. The spiced ketchup can be replaced with any other preferred sauce.

QUORN MINCE

Ingredients

KCAL 150-200

80g Cooked quorn mince

20g Diced courgette

20g Diced carrot

30g Tomato salsa

35g Grated cheddar

Chef's Tip

Making it a meal? Add onion and garlic to cook with the mince and add dried oregano for extra flavour.

LEEK AND POTATO PIE

Ingredients

KCAL
400-500

40g Leek

80g Potato

50g Cheese sauce

30g Onion

Puff/Shortcrust pastry

5g Parsley

Chef's Tip

For the best results, use grease proof paper or cling film to line the CRIMPiT to ensure a smooth removal from the device. Egg wash the top for a perfect golden CRIMPiT pie.

VEGGIE BREAKFAST

Ingredients

KCAL
400-500

70g Cooked hash brown

30g Grated cheddar cheese

40g Cooked mushrooms

60g Baked beans

Chef's Tip

You can make your own hash brown mixture by grating potato, chopping an onion and frying before adding to the recipe.

VEGGIE SAUSAGE

Ingredients

KCAL 270-320

70g Cooked veggie sausage

50g Mixed bean salad

30g Red onion

30g Goats cheese

15g Spinach

Chef's Tip

There are plenty of vegetarian protein options that can be used instead of sausages, just add your favourite.

PUMPKIN, GORGONZOLA & MAPLE

Ingredients

KCAL
300-350

80g Roast pumpkin

35g Gorgonzola

20g Rocket

20g Maple syrup

25g Pesto

Chef's Tip

Pumpkin can be replaced with any roast vegetables such as butternut squash or sweet potato.

VEGGIE MINCE

Ingredients

KCAL 320-370

100g Diced vegetables

40g Tomato pasta sauce

30g Cream cheese

30g Grated cheese

Chef's Tip

Add your favourite nuts for more protein and an extra crunch.

GOATS CHEESE & OLIVE

Ingredients

KCAL
250-300

30g Olive tapenade

20g Chopped olives

30g Cooked red pepper

30g Tomato

50g Goats cheese

20g Rocket

10g Balsamic vinegar

Chef's Tip

For a different take on this recipe, try honey and walnuts with the olive tapenade and goats cheese.

CAPRESE SALAD

Ingredients

KCAL

180-230

50g Tomato

70g Fresh mozzarella

10g Fresh basil

10g Balsamic glaze

15g Rocket

Chef's Tip

You can use a variety of tomatoes for this recipe such as vine ripened, heirloom and sweet cherry tomatoes to give this more texture.

FALAFEL

Ingredients

KCAL 550-650

65g Falafels

65g Hummus

30g Coleslaw

40g Feta

30g Sweet chilli sauce

Chef's Tip

Plenty of fresh herbs and some salad leaves will add flavour and crunch for the perfect cold crimped wrap.

ZA'ATAR SPICED HALLOUMI & TZATZIKI

Ingredients

KCAL 400-450

80g Halloumi

5g Za'atar spice

40g Tzatziki

30g Grated courgette

30g Chickpeas

Chef's Tip

You can use any dried spices to flavour the halloumi. Make your own tzatziki with yoghurt, lemon, cucumber and mint.

RAINBOW SALAD

Ingredients

KCAL 200-250

40g Grated carrot

40g Grated beetroot

40g Hummus

30g Cucumber

30g Feta

15g Spinach

Chef's Tip

If you're not a fan of beetroot, try adding chopped cabbage instead.

TEX MEX BURRITO

Ingredients

KCAL 200-250

65g Cooked peppers

10g Fajita seasoning

30g Cooked mushrooms

20g Sweetcorn

30g Grated cheddar

30 Sour cream

5g Coriander

Chef's Tip

You can replace peppers with any cooked vegetable like courgette, onions or carrot. Use cream cheese instead of sour cream if you prefer.

VEGAN

BEAN, MUSHROOM & CARAMELISED ONION

Ingredients

KCAL
190-240

60g Cooked mushrooms

40g Crushed kidney beans

30g Cooked peppers

20g Caramelised onion

15g Rocket

20g Vegan cheese

Chef's Tip

Crush the kidney bean and fry with garlic and onion, adding small amounts of water when the mix dries out. Make extra and use as a dipping sauce.

ROAST VEG & SALSA

Ingredients

50g Roasted courgette

50g Roast red pepper

50g Roast pumpkin

20g Cooked spinach

30g Tomato salsa

10g Chilli oil

5g Coriander

KCAL

380-430

Chef's Tip

The tomato salsa can be replaced with any salsa or chutney you prefer.

SPICED TOFU

Ingredients

KCAL 200-300

80g Firm tofu

5g Curry powder

15g Chopped cashews

30g Grated courgette

5g Sesame seeds

10g Spinach

25g Coconut soy yoghurt

Chef's Tip

Marinade the tofu with curry powder and some yoghurt, then pan fry or oven bake to crispen the outside to enhance flavour and texture.

MISO AUBERGINE

Ingredients

KCAL 200-250

80g Cooked aubergine

25g Miso paste, soy sauce
& sesame oil mix

20g Bean sprouts

10g Crushed peanuts

15g Spring onion

15g Kale

20g Spiced coconut yoghurt

5g Sesame seeds

Chef's Tip

Add some sliced chilli if you want added spice to this recipe.

GREEK SALAD

Ingredients

KCAL 300-350

30g Tomato

30g Olives

30g Cucumber

5g Fresh mint

30g Red onion

5g Dried oregano

10g Olive oil

40g Vegan feta

Chef's Tip

Balsamic vinegar or vegan pesto will add another level of flavour to this awesome CRIMPiT.

JACKFRUIT & MANGO CHUTNEY

Ingredients

170-220 KCAL

90g Jackfruit

30g Mango chutney

20g Mange tout

10g Spring onion

20g Coconut yoghurt

Chef's Tip

Jackfruit can be bought in tins in most supermarkets and is a great meat substitute. This combination will get anyone converted to a vegan CRIMPiT!

SPRING ROLL WRAP

Ingredients

KCAL 180-230

90g Stir fried vegetables

5g Garlic

5g Ginger

10g Soy sauce

20g Sweet chilli sauce

40g Cooked rice noodles

Chef's Tip

Use any combination of cooked noodle and vegetable mix to recreate the spring roll!

INDIAN LENTILS

Ingredients

KCAL
280-330

80g Spiced lentil

60g Onion bhaji

45g Coconut yoghurt

5g Coriander

Chef's Tip

Buy the lentils and bhajis pre-made or make your own. The longer you cook the lentils, the creamier they become.

HOISIN TOFU

Ingredients

KCAL 120-170

80g Firm tofu

25g Hoisin sauce

15g Spring onion

25g Cucumber

15g Watercress

Chef's Tip

Replace the tofu with your favourite vegan alternative and re-create an Asian style crimped wrap.

SWEET

CHOCOLATE ORANGE

Ingredients

KCAL 280-330

30g Chocolate orange

20g Mascarpone

15g Pistachio

Chef's Tip

Use your preferred chocolate to make this indulgent treat.

BLUEBERRY CHEESE CAKE

Ingredients

30g Blueberry jam

30g Cream cheese

20g Chocolate spread

KCAL 300-350

Chef's Tip

Add a touch of vanilla and lemon zest to enhance the flavour. If it's too rich, add some soured cream to tone down the sweetness.

BANOFFEE

Ingredients

KCAL
150-200

30g Banana

20g Crushed biscuit

20g Caramel sauce

Chef's Tip

Serve with ice cream and caramel sauce to spruce up this CRIMPiT.

PEANUT BUTTER & STRAWBERRIES

Ingredients

35g Peanut butter

30g Fresh strawberries

20g Cashew nuts

KCAL 300-400

Chef's Tip

Try different nut butters and different combinations of fruit and nuts to create new versions of this recipe.

APPLE AND BLACKBERRY PIE

Ingredients

KCAL 180-250

30g Apple compote

15g Blackberries

20g Vanilla custard

Chef's Tip

You will never need to make apple crumble again after you have tried a crimped apple pie! Add crushed biscuit or toasted oats for an extra crunchy texture.

MAPLE, BANANA & PEANUT

Ingredients

KCAL
150-250

30g Banana

15g Maple syrup

15g Peanuts

Chef's Tip

A great way of using up those ageing bananas, quick, easy and will still taste great.

STRAWBERRIES & WHITE CHOCOLATE

Ingredients

KCAL 230-270

30g Strawberries

30g White chocolate

10g Hazelnuts

Chef's Tip

Served with whipped cream for an elegant dessert or treat.

LEMON TART

Ingredients

25g Lemon curd

5g Crushed meringue

15g Crushed cookies

10g Raspberries

KCAL
200-300

Chef's Tip

Replace the lemon curd with your favourite jam or marmalade.

S'MORES

Ingredients

220-270 KCAL

10g Marshmallows

20g Chocolate chips

30g Crushed biscuits

Chef's Tip

Use small marshmallows or chop up big ones so they melt quicker and give even consistency.

RASPBERRIES & VANILLA MASCARPONE

Ingredients

15g Raspberry jam

20g Raspberries

30g Vanilla Mascarpone

20g Chocolate spread

KCAL

300-350

Chef's Tip

Mascarpone cheese mixed with vanilla and icing sugar makes a delicious filling to go with fruit and chocolate.